Just say the word "DOLPHIN" and watch how people smile. Dolphins have a special charm. It's not just their **beauty** or their **intelligence**. It's not just their **mysterious** lives in a world of water as alien to us as outer space. It's something I've felt from the moment I first saw one. It's a kind of magic, **dolphin magic**. Come with me and feel its spell for yourself.

Wild About
Dolphins

by
Nicola Davies

CANDLEWICK PRESS
CAMBRIDGE, MASSACHUSETTS

CONTENTS

"'Dolphins!' I yelled." PAGE 20

"They came so close that I could see their dark eyes looking up at us." PAGE 14

PAGE 29

"How they leapt! High above the water. Spinning so fast their bodies blurred with speed."

"Each baby swam just below its mom's tummy . . . as if tied by an invisible string." PAGE 38

"All that summer
we ran into
dolphins."
PAGE 22

"I kept watch as we sped along.
Then I heard 'pfff, pfff.'"
PAGE 42

I was very small when I saw my first dolphins. They leapt through hoops, right in front of my wide eyes.

"Big fish!" I said to my dad.

"Not fish, sweetie," he told me. "They're **bottlenose dolphins**. All dolphins are mammals. They live in the sea but they breathe air, like we do."

The dolphins jumped so high and swam so fast, I was enchanted. I imagined them leaping through waves, not hoops. I decided that one day I would meet them in the wild, where they belonged.

Chapter One

LOOKING FOR
DOLPHINS

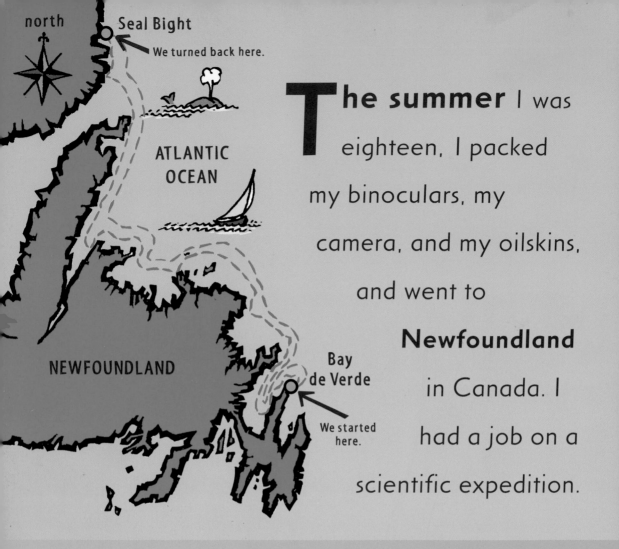

north

Seal Bight
We turned back here.

ATLANTIC
OCEAN

NEWFOUNDLAND

Bay
de Verde

We started
here.

The **summer** I was eighteen, I packed my binoculars, my camera, and my oilskins, and went to **Newfoundland** in Canada. I had a job on a scientific expedition.

By the time I got to Newfoundland, I'd read a lot about dolphins. I knew they are part of a group of mammals called cetaceans (SE-TAY-SHENS). It includes whales, porpoises, and dolphins.

I also knew there are lots of species of dolphin. They all have the same basic body plan. →

MELON: a pad of fat over the forehead. Helps dolphins to send out sounds underwater.

BLOWHOLE: the nostril, for breathing. It is closed underwater and opens at the surface.

BEAK: long jaws with lots of teeth. Good for grabbing squid and other slippery prey.

8

It was a voyage along the coast, in a boat called *Firenze*, to count dolphins and whales.

The waters off Newfoundland are cold enough for icebergs, but full of life. In summer there are huge shoals of fish and squid. Whales and dolphins come to feast on them.

My job was to help sail *Firenze* and keep records of what we saw. But all I really wanted was to feel that **dolphin magic** again.

DORSAL FIN: helps to stop the dolphin rolling from side to side. Shape and size vary from species to species.

TAIL FLUKES: for swimming. Beat up and down to push the dolphin along.

FLIPPERS: help to steer. Inside, they have bones just like human hands.

The **expedition leaders** were Kath and Patty. They could steer a boat, mend a sail, sing a shanty, and cook dinner

Patty

all at once. They were tough and funny and kind, and they taught me how to look for dolphins.

"Calm days are best," said Kath. "You can see their fins cut through the surface."

"Morning and evening are best," said Patty. "When the sun is low and the light slants over the water, it picks out their backs."

"But you can see them anytime," said Kath.

Kath

10

You only get to see dolphins when they come to the surface to breathe. Kath and Patty told me what to look for.

DORSAL FINS → usually triangular but curved — different **species** have differently shaped fins.

ACROBATICS

porpoising (traveling along in and out of the water)

jumps (right out of the water)

spyhops (head out, to have a look around)

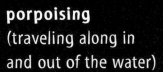

BLOWS
puffs of air and water spray, like a whale makes as it breathes out, but much smaller — sometimes just bubbles.

WARNING: bad weather and high waves make these glimpses of dolphins harder to spot.

So from HORIZON to HORIZON, from dawn to dusk,

in calm and storm, I looked out.

And still when I saw
my first dolphins, it was a **surprise**.

One moment the sea was green
and clear, and empty as a pane of glass.
The next, six dolphins were riding a wave,
like figures held inside a paperweight.

Their swimming seemed effortless. In a moment, with just a flick of their tail flukes, they were dodging under our boat. They came so close that I could see their dark eyes looking up at us. I found that I was tingling with excitement, every hair on end!

They didn't look like the dolphins I had seen

HOW DO DOLPHINS SWIM SO FAST?

Kath told me that scientists don't fully understand how dolphins swim so fast. But here are some clues.

They have a streamlined shape that moves through the water with barely a ripple.

Their skin is incredibly smooth, too. It sheds up to 12 times a day to keep as slippery as wet soap.

in the zoo. These dolphins had short beaks, and fins curved like fat sickles on their backs. Their bodies were streaked with gray, white, and yellow.

"They're **white-sided dolphins**," said Patty.

"Hey," said Kath, "the wind's coming up. Let's put on some speed and see what they do!"

Huge back muscles move the tail flukes up and down. This powers the dolphin's body through the water.

Part of our job was to record which species we saw. To make sure we had identified a dolphin correctly, we looked up a checklist of key features.

ATLANTIC WHITE-SIDED DOLPHIN

SIZE: between 8 and 9 feet long

FOUND: in cool water in the North Atlantic

POD: between 5 and 50 animals per pod (a pod is a herd or family group of cetaceans)

Firenze leapt along, pushed faster and faster by the wind. Instantly, the dolphins caught up, then zipped in front and played around our **bows**. They seemed to take turns at it.

Leaning over the bows, I could see their

blowholes when they came up for air, and hear the soft **"pfff"** of their breath. Then, in just a heartbeat, they broke away into the green water and were gone.

"Maybe they're following a shoal of fish," said Patty.

"Yeah," said Kath, "that's why we see them close to land in summer. Lots of fish come up from deep water when the shallows warm up."

The bow is the pointed front end of the boat (and rhymes with "wow," not "slow"). On bigger, faster boats, the bow makes waves big enough for dolphins to surf on. This is called bow riding, and dolphins do it for one reason: FUN!

HOW DO BLOWHOLES WORK?

The blowhole is on top of the head, and dolphins can't see it break the surface. So how do they know when to open it to breathe? Patty said the skin around the blowhole is so sensitive, dolphins can **feel** when it is breaking the surface. Then they open the blowhole, take quick breaths, and dive again. For deep dives, some dolphins can hold their breath for 15 minutes!

I longed for the dolphins to come back, but a storm was brewing and we had to find shelter from the roar of the wind and the waves.

We dropped anchor in the shelter of a bay. The air was so quiet it was easy to hear that sound again:

"pfff."

The water was smooth as glass, so it was easy to see four black backs at the surface. They looked like rubber tubes rolling through the water.

HOW DO YOU TELL A DOLPHIN FROM A PORPOISE? Porpoises are cetaceans, like dolphins, but they are a different family. They're smaller and rounder, and they have a small triangular fin. There are six species, but the one we saw, the harbor porpoise, is the only one in this part of the Atlantic.

"Dolphins!"

I said.

"No," said Kath. "Those are **harbor porpoises**. They like these quiet little coves, but they don't like boats. They won't stick around now that we're here!"

"They'll be off to feed on little fish and shrimps down on the bottom of the bay," said Patty. "I'm going below to cook supper."

HARBOR PORPOISE

SIZE: 4$\frac{1}{2}$–6 feet

FOUND: in the North Atlantic, Pacific, and Arctic oceans

POD: 2–5

WHAT ABOUT WHALES?
The word "whale" is often used to mean the bigger species of cetacean, like these two killer whales or orcas. But big species and small species (like dolphins and porpoises) can all be called whales because they are all cetaceans.

Next time I saw dolphins, I was ready. I spotted the sickle-shaped dorsal fins, the flashes of white flanks.

"Dolphins!" I yelled. "White-sided!"

"No," said Kath, "those are **white-beaked** dolphins."

"See the way the white patch goes up over the back?" said Patty. "That's how you know them. They don't always have white beaks."

Suddenly, two leapt up together, turned in the air, and slapped down on their backs. The splash wet our deck, they were so close.

Close enough to see their patterns, but too close for me to be able to speak.

WHITE-BEAKED DOLPHIN

SIZE: 8–9 feet

FOUND: in cool water in the North Atlantic Ocean

POD: 2–30

HOW DO DOLPHINS JUMP SO HIGH?

Try jumping out of the water next time you're swimming, without pushing off from the bottom. It's impossible!

Dolphins do it by swimming very fast just under the surface, then turning suddenly so their speed carries them up into the air. Or by coming straight up from deep water like a rocket. We can't swim fast enough for that!

All that **summer** we ran into dolphins. And every time we did, I learned a little more about watching them. How to tell how many were in each group . . .

How to tell the different species apart . . .

How to spot which dolphins had been in fights, or attacked by sharks and orcas . . .

But often all we saw was a glimpse of back and then all we could say was,

Groups of dolphins are hard to count. For every dolphin you see, there might be another one underwater. We did our best to guess how many at a time came to the surface, then doubled it. Or we took a photo and counted later. Once we counted 124 white-beaks in a picture, so the group (or pod) may have contained more than 200!

"There's a dolphin!"

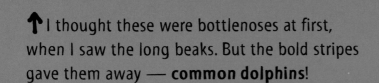

COMMON DOLPHIN

SIZE: 5^1/$_2$–8 feet

FOUND: in cool and warm waters worldwide

POD: 10–500

↑ I thought these were bottlenoses at first, when I saw the long beaks. But the bold stripes gave them away — **common dolphins**!

RISSO'S DOLPHIN

SIZE: 8^1/$_2$–12^1/$_2$ feet

FOUND: in cool and warm waters worldwide

POD: 3–50

← Kath yelled "GRAMPUS!" when she saw these. It's another name for **Risso's dolphins**. Accidental scratches or toothmarks from fights with other Risso's dolphins heal as white scars. As the dolphins get older, they get more and more scars.

23

The summer is short in Newfoundland. In September, sky and sea turned gray, and the first storms of winter blew down from the Arctic. Fish and dolphins headed for the safety of deeper water far from land. We'd finished our survey, from south to north and back again.

It was time to go. I helped to get *Firenze* out of the water and into dry dock for the winter. Then I said goodbye to Patty and Kath and flew home. I wondered when we'd sail with dolphins again.

Chapter Two

SWIMMING WITH
DOLPHINS

north

INDIA

INDIAN
OCEAN

SRI LANKA

Trincomalee

Male

MALDIVES

In less than a year I got a call from Patty and Kath. "We're off to sea again. Come with us!" This time we were aboard a sailing boat called *Elendil.* We were far from any coast, counting cetaceans in the middle of the **Indian Ocean**. The water was as warm as a bath, as blue as an angel's eyes.

I was on dolphin lookout. I spent days up the mast, watching, but I saw nothing.

From here I could see farther, and right down into the water. The Indian Ocean was so clear, it made the Atlantic seem like soup.

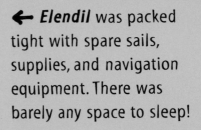

← *Elendil* was packed tight with spare sails, supplies, and navigation equipment. There was barely any space to sleep!

↑ **Sometimes flying fish landed on our decks.** Their "wings" are really extra-big fins. Some species have two, and some have four. They jump from the water and glide over the surface to escape from predators.

Patty hoisted meals up to me on a rope.

"See anything?"

"Flying fish. Driftwood. That's all."

Then one afternoon the smooth water exploded into life. Dolphins burst through the surface, twenty, thirty, forty at once.

They were dark gray and slender, skinny almost, with long, pointed snouts.

These spinners have the longest, skinniest beak of any dolphin. No wonder they're called long-snouts! They dive deep to catch fish and squid, usually at night. Maybe a long beak is good for grabbing prey in the dark.

"Spinner dolphins," Kath called up. How they leapt! High above the water. Spinning so fast their bodies blurred with speed. We watched them pass into the distance, still leaping.

LONG-SNOUTED SPINNER DOLPHIN

SIZE: 4–8 feet

FOUND: in all warm waters, mostly far out to sea

POD: up to 1,000!

I asked Patty why dolphins leap. She said no one really knows. Some say it's to shake off any dirt or tiny creatures clinging to their skin, and keep it silky smooth. It could be to make a noisy splash underwater, or prove to other dolphins that they are fit and strong. Patty reckons it's just for fun.

For days after that, the sea seemed especially empty. I got so gloomy that one evening Kath said, "We can **hear** dolphins even if we can't see them."

She put the underwater microphone over the side of

the boat. We all took turns to listen on the headphones. I never knew it was so noisy under the sea! It sounded like a huge busy kitchen!

Kath and Patty saw my face and laughed. They'd heard the sounds before.

"The noise like bacon frying is shrimps," said Patty.

"I can hear kettles whistling and plates chinking," I said.

"Dolphins, hunting!" they chorused.

"They could be a mile away," said Kath. "Sound travels farther underwater."

"Or they could be right underneath us," said Patty, "eating squid dinners!"

I went on listening long into the night. Staring down into the water, I imagined the dolphins'

Kath said dolphins do a lot of their hunting at night, in the dark. Even by day, underwater light is dim. Their eyes can make the most of tiny amounts of light. But dolphins rely on excellent hearing to find food and each other.

With dolphins, the earhole is just a tiny hole, and it's plugged with wax. So they don't hear much through there. Instead, sounds travel through a special piece of their jaw that connects with each ear on the inside.

dark world, full of sounds. By dawn the sounds had faded, and the dolphins were far away.

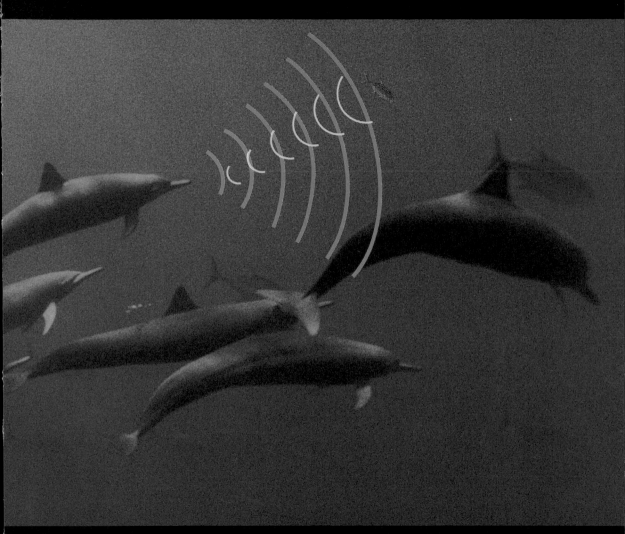

Dolphins make a lot of noise! Whistles to keep in touch, and clicks for hunting. The clicks are part of their echolocation system. The melon beams the clicks ahead. They bounce off what's out there and come back as echoes.

This is dolphin sonar, a sound map of their world, food included! But dolphins can also **feel** where their food is. Their skin is very sensitive, especially around the jaws. So they can feel the tiny waves that fish or squid make when they are close by.

The bright blue sky stretched over an empty sea again. Then suddenly something new leapt from the water.

A huge fish, fat and silvered. Then another, and another. Each one more than three feet long.

"Tuna!" I called down,

"And **spotted dolphins**!" Kath yelled back. "Look, some of them are just babies!"

In moments the boat was surrounded by hundreds of leaping dolphins and their calves.

Spotted dolphins are often seen with yellowfin tuna because they feed on the same fish and squid, close to the surface. Dolphins often get caught in the nets of tuna fishermen, and drown. Nowadays, fishermen take more care to release the dolphins, so fewer die.

"Why don't you two get in with them?" said Kath, "I'll stay aboard and steer."

Go swimming with dolphins? That's like having a dream come true. We didn't need to be asked twice!

We struggled into masks, snorkels, and flippers, then climbed down into the water. We hung on to a rope so that we could drift behind *Elendil*, among the dolphins.

Under the surface we were in the dolphins' world. Living so far from land, these dolphins might never have seen humans before. We must have seemed strange to them, dangling on our rope.

They came close to investigate. They swam beside us, under us, behind us, using their sonar to try and figure out what we were. Their clicks went through my body like a shiver.

They looked at us so intently. Staring out through my mask, my eyes met the eyes of dolphins. There it was again: the tingle of magic.

The mothers with calves were wary and hung back. Each baby swam just below its mom's tummy, or just above her, as if tied by an invisible string. Some of them were so small I could have cradled them in my arms.

Newborn spotted dolphins have no spots. The babies get their first spots after about a year, on their tummies. By the time they are grown up, at 9 to 12 years, they have lots!

PANTROPICAL SPOTTED DOLPHIN

SIZE: 5½–7½ feet

FOUND: in warm waters worldwide

POD: 50–3,000

Spot the difference? The spotted dolphin photos on pages 36–39 show the Atlantic species. There are hardly any underwater photos of the Pantropical species that we saw. We were lucky to get close!

← TOGETHERNESS

Dolphins like to be together. They touch each other a lot and play, even when they have grown up. But moms and dads don't stay together after mating. Males don't take part in rearing the young.

The moms aren't all alone. Other female dolphins help. At the birth, they may crowd around the mother to protect her and hold her up in the water.

BIRTH

Dolphins have just one baby at a time, after about a year of pregnancy. First the tail comes out, then the rest of the body, then the head. Then the little calf swims like mad to the surface to take its first breath — sometimes with a nudge from Mom or an aunt.

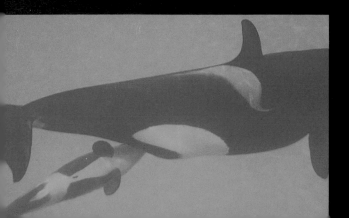

← FEEDING TIME

Dolphin babies suckle milk from their mothers' teats, like other mammals do. Orca calves suckle for nearly two years and stay close to Mom all the time. It's probably similar in other dolphins too.

Then quite suddenly the dolphins grew tired of us and swam on faster than we could sail.

Joyful, half-drowned, Patty and I crawled onto the deck.

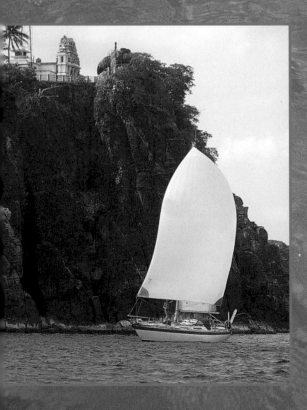

"Dolphins," she yelled over the side, "I love you!"

The next day we sighted land. It meant that our journey was nearly over.

We left the angel-eyed
ocean and slipped sadly
back to the coast. It was
time to drop anchor and
say goodbye to *Elendil*.
We put the sails away,
packed up our gear, and
rowed ashore.

Later, we sat on the harbor wall, glum
and silent. We were all going home
to different places. Would we ever sail on
dolphin seas again?

Then Patty said, "Let's pretend we're rich and
plan another trip. A round-the-world voyage to
see all the dolphins we've never seen!"

"Yeah!" we all said. "Where will we start?"

In ten minutes, Kath and Patty had planned our dolphin-watching route around the globe. When they asked me what I wanted to see, I could think of only one thing.

"I want to see the dolphins I saw in the zoo when I was little."

"Bottlenose dolphins?"

"They're almost everywhere. Funny we never saw them on this trip."

"Oh, we'll see them for sure!"

We sat on the harbor wall so long ago. Mostly I don't think about it, but today I remembered it all. At the end of a vacation in the Caribbean, I decided to take a trip on a boat. I kept watch as we sped along. Then I heard **"pfff, pfff."**

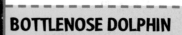

BOTTLENOSE DOLPHIN

SIZE: 6–13 feet

FOUND: in warm and cool waters all over the world. Usually close to coasts, even in harbors and estuaries.

POD: 1–10

I looked down. Bow riding at the place where our two worlds almost meet were three bottlenose dolphins!

One looked up through the water.

Maybe it saw my smile, rather like its own.

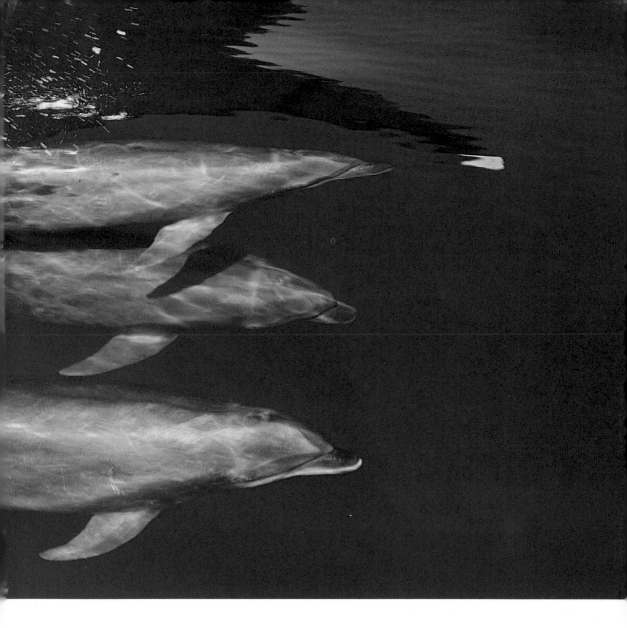

I'd met my dolphins, wild in the ocean at last.

I thought about my dad then, and Patty and

Kath, and the round-the-world voyage that

we never made.

At least, not yet!

A guide to dolphin species

We saw seven species of dolphins, but there are many more to look out for. The thirty-one species that we call dolphins are listed here. Twenty-six of these are oceanic dolphins and are divided into "beaked" and "non-beaked" species.

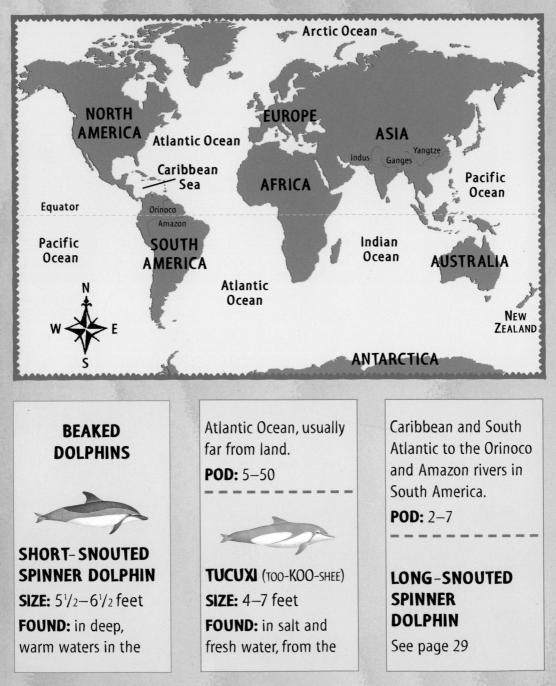

Arctic Ocean

NORTH AMERICA

Atlantic Ocean

Caribbean Sea

EUROPE

ASIA

Indus Ganges Yangtze

Pacific Ocean

AFRICA

Equator

Orinoco

Amazon

Pacific Ocean

SOUTH AMERICA

Indian Ocean

AUSTRALIA

Atlantic Ocean

N W E S

NEW ZEALAND

ANTARCTICA

BEAKED DOLPHINS

SHORT-SNOUTED SPINNER DOLPHIN

SIZE: 5½–6½ feet

FOUND: in deep, warm waters in the

Atlantic Ocean, usually far from land.

POD: 5–50

- - - - - - - - - - - -

TUCUXI (TOO-KOO-SHEE)

SIZE: 4–7 feet

FOUND: in salt and fresh water, from the

Caribbean and South Atlantic to the Orinoco and Amazon rivers in South America.

POD: 2–7

- - - - - - - - - - - -

LONG-SNOUTED SPINNER DOLPHIN

See page 29

PANTROPICAL SPOTTED DOLPHIN

See page 38

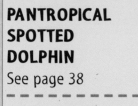

ATLANTIC SPOTTED DOLPHIN

SIZE: 5$\frac{1}{2}$–7$\frac{1}{2}$ feet

FOUND: in warm waters of the Atlantic, especially in the western Atlantic and the Caribbean.

POD: 5–15

COMMON DOLPHIN

See page 23

STRIPED DOLPHIN

SIZE: 6–8 feet

FOUND: in warm waters worldwide, usually far from land and in deep water.

POD: 10–500

ATLANTIC HUMP-BACKED DOLPHIN

SIZE: 6$\frac{1}{2}$–9 feet

FOUND: in warm shallow waters along the west coast of Africa.

POD: 3–7

ROUGH-TOOTHED DOLPHIN

SIZE: 7–9 feet

FOUND: in deep, warm waters far from land, worldwide. Little is known about this rarely seen species.

POD: 2–20

SOUTHERN RIGHT WHALE DOLPHIN

SIZE: 6–9$\frac{1}{2}$ feet

FOUND: in very cold, deep waters in the southern hemisphere. It's graceful, fast, and has no dorsal fin.

POD: 2–100

NORTHERN RIGHT WHALE DOLPHIN

SIZE: 6$\frac{1}{2}$–10 feet

FOUND: in deep, cold waters of the north Pacific, usually far from land.

POD: 5–200

INDO-PACIFIC HUMP-BACKED DOLPHIN

SIZE: 6$\frac{1}{2}$–10 feet

FOUND: in warm, shallow waters along coasts from east Africa to Australia.

POD: 3–7

BOTTLENOSE DOLPHIN See page 43

NON-BEAKED DOLPHINS

These dolphins do have beaks, but much shorter ones!

HECTOR'S DOLPHIN

SIZE: 4–5 feet

FOUND: only around the coast of New Zealand. Likes shallow water close to the shore.

POD: 2–8

BLACK DOLPHIN

SIZE: 4–5½ feet

FOUND: in cold, shallow waters around the west coast of South America. Likes to be among the waves close to shore.

POD: 2–15

COMMERSON'S DOLPHIN

SIZE: 4–5½ feet

FOUND: in cold coastal waters around the tip of South America. Likes bays, fjords, and estuaries.

POD: 1–10

HEAVISIDE'S DOLPHIN

SIZE: 5–5½ feet

FOUND: in cool shallow water only off the southwest coast of Africa.

POD: 2–3

HOURGLASS DOLPHIN

SIZE: 5–6 feet

FOUND: in the cold, remote waters of the Antarctic Ocean, often far out to sea.

POD: 1–7

DUSKY DOLPHIN

SIZE: 5–7 feet

FOUND: in cool coastal waters off South America, South Africa, and New Zealand. Comes close to boats and people.

POD: 20–500

PEALE'S DOLPHIN

SIZE: 6½–7 feet

FOUND: only around the southern coast of South America, in cool waters, often in bays and fjords.

POD: 3–8

PACIFIC WHITE-SIDED DOLPHIN

SIZE: 5½–8 feet

FOUND: in deep, cool and cold waters of the north Pacific, usually far from land.

POD: 10–100

FRASER'S DOLPHIN

SIZE: 6½–8½ feet

FOUND: only in warm, deep oceanic waters. Most common in the eastern Pacific, but also off Sri Lanka, South Africa, and the Caribbean.

POD: 100–500

IRRAWADDY DOLPHIN

SIZE: 7–8½ feet

FOUND: in warm shallow waters close to shore, from India to northern Australia. Likes estuaries and mangrove swamps. Travels more than 620 miles up some rivers.

POD: 1–7

WHITE-BEAKED DOLPHIN

See page 20

ATLANTIC WHITE-

SIDED DOLPHIN

See page 15

RISSO'S DOLPHIN (GRAMPUS)

See page 23

RIVER DOLPHINS

These belong to a different family from the others. They are generally smaller and slower, with long beaks and tiny eyes.

FRANCISCANA

SIZE: 4–5½ feet

FOUND: in the cool waters off the south-eastern coast of South America. The only river dolphin that doesn't live in a river!

POD: 1–5

BAIJI

SIZE: 4½–8 feet

FOUND: along the Yangtze River in China.

Very shy, and so rare that it is an endangered species.

POD: 3–6

INDUS & GANGES RIVER DOLPHINS

SIZE: 5–8 feet

FOUND: these two very similar species, one in the Indus, the other in the Ganges, like the muddiest part of their rivers. They are almost blind, and find their way by echolocation.

POD: 1–2

BOTO

SIZE: 6–9 feet

FOUND: in the great Orinoco and Amazon rivers of South America. In the wet season, when the forests flood, Botos leave the rivers and swim among the trees!

POD: 1–10

Why we count dolphins

We need to know more about
dolphins so that we can try to protect them.

Dolphins are trapped in fishing nets and poisoned by pollution. But it's hard to tell how bad the effects are without knowing the answers to some simple questions.
How many dolphins are there?
Where do they live?
What do they eat?
How often do they breed?

All over the world, research expeditions like ours are finding answers to questions like these. Identifying species and counting individuals are the first steps. Once you know where to find dolphins, you can go back to these areas and try to find out more!

We have a lot to learn about dolphins. But here are some of the questions that we know the answers to. (Of course, there are more dolphin answers all through this book!)

★ Are dolphins endangered?

At the moment, four species are on the endangered list: the Baiji, Ganges and Indus river dolphins, and Hector's dolphin.

★ Which is the rarest dolphin?

Some species seem rare because they are hard to see, like the rough-toothed dolphin. Or they are found in only one place, like Heaviside's dolphin. The rarest is the Baiji. There are fewer than 200 left, because pollution and dams have destroyed their river habitat.

★ How long do dolphins live?

We're not sure how long most species can live in the wild. In captivity, some bottlenose dolphins live for 25 to 30 years.

★ Do dolphins know where they are going?

Yes! One bit of sea can look much like another, but dolphins have to know where they can find food, safety, and each other.

Dolphins can use sight and echolocation only over a short distance. Over long distances, they may listen out for clues like the sound of waves on the shore, or other animals' calls.

It seems dolphins also have a kind of built-in compass in their brains, to help them navigate across the ocean.

⭐ Is it true that dolphins rescue people?

Some people think so. But a dolphin can look as if it's holding up a drowning swimmer or a sinking boat when it's just being playful.

⭐ Do dolphins have a language?

Dolphins can learn to use a sign language taught to them by humans. But we still don't understand how dolphins communicate with their own sounds. We do know that some whistles, called signature whistles, identify individual dolphins like a name.

⭐ Are dolphins very clever?

Intelligence tests show that dolphins can learn tricks about as well as a smart dog. But what does intelligence really mean? Dolphins are brilliant at what they do best — being dolphins!

Find out more

These conservation groups can help you find out more about protecting dolphins and other ocean life.

GREENPEACE
- UK:
Canonbury Villas
London N1 2PN
- USA:
702 H St. NW
Washington, DC
20001
- Australia:
Level 4
35–39 Liverpool St.
Sydney NSW 2000
- www.greenpeace.org

IFAW (International Fund for Animal Welfare)
www.ifaw.org

THE WORLD CONSERVATION INSTITUTE / THE OCEAN ALLIANCE
191 Western Road
Lincoln, MA 01773
www.oceanalliance.org

INTERNATIONAL WILDLIFE COALITION
70 E. Falmouth Hwy.
E. Falmouth, MA
02536
www.iwc.org

WWF (World Wildlife Fund)
- UK:
Panda House
Weyside Park
Godalming GU7 1XR
- USA:
1250 24th St. NW
Washington, DC
20037
- Australia:
Level 5
725 George St.
Sydney NSW 2000

CETACEA
www.cetacea.org/ dolphins.htm

Acknowledgments

PHOTOGRAPHS

Heather Angel: 6, 11t ➤ ARDEA London: François Gohier 16, 22, 23t; Denise Herzing 39t
Aspect Pictures Ltd: 7t, 25t, 40 ➤ Robin W. Baird: 14–15, 18t
Nicola Davies: 3, 7b, 10t, 24, 25b, 26, 41 ➤ Jonathan Gordon: 27l, 30, 40b ➤ Pam Kemp: 28t, 29r
Marine Mammal Images: James Watt 11cl, 35; Eda Rogers 39b ➤ Oxford Scientific Film: 17, 28b, 44–45
Planet Earth Pictures: cover, 11c, 11cr, 18b, 27r, 34, 36–37, 38 ➤ PPL: cover, 30–31, 43, back cover
RSPCA Photolibrary: Rick Rosenthal 32–33 ➤ Richard Sears-MICS: 21
Still Pictures: Doug Perrine 2; Roland Seitre 12–13, 23b, 28–29, 54–55; Mark Carwardine cover, 20
Paul Thompson: 11b ➤ Hal Whitehead: 10b

ILLUSTRATIONS

Claire Melinsky: 8–9, 14–15, 26, 39 ➤ Mike Bostock: 46–49

Consultant: **Dr. Jonathan Gordon**   Editor: **Camilla Hallinan**   Designer: **Louise Jackson**

Text copyright © 2001 by Nicola Davies
Illustrations copyright © 2001 by Walker Books Ltd.
All rights reserved.
First U. S. edition 2001
Library of Congress Cataloging-in-Publication Data is available.
Library of Congress Catalog Card Number 00-065197
ISBN 0-7636-1454-8
2 4 6 8 10 9 7 5 3 1
Printed in Hong Kong
This book was typeset in Letraset Arta and Myriad Tilt.
Candlewick Press
2067 Massachusetts Avenue
Cambridge, Massachusetts 02140
visit us at www.candlewick.com

For Hal, Patty, Kath, Jonathan, Gay, Phil, Vassilli, and all the children of *Firenze* and *Elendil*. N. D.